THE BIGGER WORLD

THE
BIGGER
WORLD

THE CHARACTER
POEMS OF

NOELLE
KOCOT

WAVE BOOKS   SEATTLE

AND NEW YORK

Published by Wave Books

www.wavepoetry.com

Copyright © 2011 by Noelle Kocot
Wave Books titles are distributed to the trade by
Consortium Book Sales and Distribution
Phone: 800-283-3572 / SAN 631-760X

This title is available in limited edition hardcover
directly from the publisher

Library of Congress Cataloging-in-Publication Data
Kocot, Noelle.
The bigger world : the character poems
of Noelle Kocot. — 1st ed.
p.   cm.
ISBN 978-1-933517-52-0 (pbk. : alk. paper)
I. Title.
PS3611.O36B54 2011
811'.6—dc22
2010034253

Designed and composed by Quemadura
Printed in the United States of America

9 8 7 6 5 4 3 2 1

First Edition

Wave Books 028

CONTENTS

God Bless the Child 1

The West Village 3

Life on the Mountain 5

Noneness 7

Book of Life 9

Homage 11

It Was Freedom 13

Fugue 15

Gnomon 17

Pandora 18

No One Would Be Home 20

Persepolis 22

Pharaoh 23

Fourth of July 24

Welcome Mat 26

On Becoming a Person 28

Era 30

Red-Eye 32

Favors from the Dead 34

Unanswered Question 37

Homage 39

Ballad 40

Rainbow Lanes 42

A Suburban Tale 44

The Love That Lasts After Death 47

Daniel 50

The Cetacean Society 52

The IRS 54

In Sickness 57

True Story 59

Aunt Lee Watches the First Snow 61

The Last Time She Saw Him 63

Marie 66

Love Story 68

Kind Regards 70

Sandy's Heroin 72

Circle of Life 73

THE BIGGER WORLD

GOD BLESS
THE CHILD

Horatia hated children,
Fat children, short children,
Tall children, small children,
Skinny children, long children,
Any type of children, she despised,
And avoided them completely.
If a child was to be at a gathering,
She wouldn't go. If one of her
Friends had a child, she'd stop
Talking to her. Then Horatia became
Pregnant and gave birth to a full-
Grown man. It was an easy birth,
Despite what people believed.
The man, her son, proved to be

A good and loyal son, and when
Horatia got old, he was there
At her side, playing mahjong
With her, taking her for walks.
Once when they were walking,
Horatia was met by a sea of children
In summer camp tee shirts. They
Smelled so good, and seemed so happy.
She was so overwhelmed that
She started to cry. "Is this what
I've been avoiding?" Horatia asked
Herself silently. Her son, who looked
Her age now, noticed her tears and said,
"Mother, I do believe that you never
Once allowed me to be a child,
But I forgive you, seeing as how you
Were never really a child yourself."
Horatia felt at peace, finally, after so
Many years of bottled-up hatred
And fear. She and her son walked
Silently on, not out of the flames
Or anything, but just walked on.

THE WEST VILLAGE

Jelka awoke like a sunflower.
"I always said I'd give a body
Part to live on Bleecker Street
And now I'm giving one
And getting one!" Jelka had
Just married Soren, a doctor
She'd known for about ten days.
He'd touch her tongue with
His stethoscope and found
The beating of an open heart,
Redolent of the spring. When
Soren said the magic word,
Jelka was obsessed. "Cheese-
Cake!" Jelka beamed, "I do."
Jelka and Soren spent their
Honeymoon in a cave, and

Watched things thaw. When
They returned to their nest,
Soren presented Jelka with
The gift of an MRI machine.
"But honey, I'm terrified
Of enclosed spaces." Soren
Reassured her and coaxed
Her in. Jelka was pleased
And stayed inside for days.
The days turned to weeks,
And Soren became concerned.
One day, months later, Jelka
Emerged. She had lived solely
Off of her vast body fat. Now
That she was thin, Soren
Didn't love her anymore.
Yet he stayed with her and gave
Her sunflowers every day,
And they lived together as
Husband and wife, in the land
Of Nod, while their building
Flapped in the wind like a lung.

LIFE ON THE
MOUNTAIN

Todd promised Francine,
"I will make you very happy."
But Francine didn't want happiness,
She wanted truth, which was savage
And dangerous. "I want a solution
For my disease," said Francine,
"And I want it quick." So Todd
Went to the witch doctor, and came
Back with the cure. "Boil this root
Until it shrivels. Make a poultice
And put it on your eyes." Francine
Did it. The giant anaconda that
Had been chasing her dissolved.
Now that she could see truth,

Happiness also came her way.
Francine married Todd, and they
Had a lot of good years together,
And every time that giant anaconda
Came back, Todd would boil
Roots for her, put them gently
On her eyes. Their memories
Were both misty and watercolored,
Through the patchwork of Francine's
Dark thoughts hovering idly by.

NONENESS

Seymour left the beach and traveled
Down a dirt road. He met a naked
Nun, and said, "Hey, what kind of
Dominoes are you slicing?" The nun
Was solemn, even though she was
Naked. She proceeded to sing
A tortured love song about her husband,
Who died before she entered the convent.
Seymour was bored. He wished
The nun was not a nun, but merely
A naked woman without nun-ness.
He ran away from the nun, who was
Still singing, and ran smack into
A railroad of infirmity. A bird with one
Leg stopped for coffee, then flew
To the railroad to greet Seymour,

Who was his oldest friend. "We are
Drifting toward, drifting away from,
Eternity," the bird warned. "I've seen
A lost civilization, some prayer beads,
And I felt an immense calm. Seymour,
You have yet to be saved, from what
I don't know." Seymour basked in
The magical light which was growing
Dimmer by the minute. The nun crawled
Off somewhere and died, and when
Her body was found, all anyone knew
About her was that she was a naked
Woman. A lazy happiness overcame
Seymour, and the bird felt content.
Hours passed like this, then days,
Then months, until they were frozen
With winter in an unknown land.

BOOK OF LIFE

The phoenix rose from the ashes
And decided to keep rising.
A forgetful monk basked in its shadow.
"Bananas taste expensive!" exclaimed
The monk, to no one in particular.
Suddenly, the phoenix swooped down
And landed on top of his head.
"I am no longer wedded to Eros,"
The phoenix warbled, "and I'd like
To live with you in the monastery,
Though my wings are still singed
And I only eat live things."
The monk rifled through his powerpack
And pulled out a squirming worm.
"Here you go, my fiery friend,
Take it and eat it, and do not worry

About the other monks, they
Mean no harm. You are to go back
To the monastery with me."
The phoenix flapped its wings
With happiness. But seemingly
Out of nowhere, the phoenix
Drilled a hole in the ground with its beak
And descended into the core of the earth.
The monk was sad and alone,
But since he was forgetful,
The memory of the phoenix soon faded.
He hummed "The Lion Sleeps Tonight"
On his way back to the other monks,
With a dim recollection of his
Younger years, when Eros lorded
Over him, and he was happy.
When he returned to the monastery,
He died of a fatally broken heart,
Not remembering exactly why.

HOMAGE

Rick was a polyamorous shaman,
Who moonlighted as a detective.
He had quite a lot of women,
All over the country. Rick
Liked to hunt wild mushrooms
In the starlight. Once he saw
Two giraffes with necks intertwined,
And he thought, "How nice would
It be if there were three, or even
Five!" Rick traversed many lands,
And he also traversed the red
Acres of language in the form
Of many books. He liked to read
Cookbooks, mainly, because he
Enjoyed looking at the pictures,
Especially cookbooks with a lot

Of mushrooms. Once when one
Of Rick's women started blubbering,
He blew pipe smoke on a tiny bug.
"Ha! This rigid pantomime has
Got to end. The solitary tear
Of a good drama is one thing,
But this is quite another!" And
So the woman stopped, and she
Snuggled up to Rick. Their lungs
Filled with air, as they listened to
The song of the blue blue warmth.

IT WAS FREEDOM

"When it's gone, who's there,
Nobody's there." This is what
Zeke believed. He began walking
In the direction of never coming
Back. His hands were stiff
And smiling, but his heart raced.
His eyes burned with the speed
Of light. Zeke needed discipline,
But unfortunately, there was no one
Around to give it. The angel
Of history? Zeke couldn't afford
Anything, but wanted people to
Think he could. He had no children
But wanted six. He walked on,
And couldn't afford to get lost
Because there'd be no one to

Go after him, to find him. The
Thing had been like a tornado
Through his life. The thing was
Hot on his ass, the thing made
Him sweat at night, and now the
Thing was his only friend.
Not one of his friends, but the only.
The only crying that Zeke ever
Heard anymore was the howling
Of the wind through the March trees,
And he relished it, it was freedom.

FUGUE

A flash of sudden joy
From the solar plexus,
Where fear usually resides.
She knew she'd be okay.
"There is no other life
Apart from this one," she
Said to no one in particular.
The building gleamed
In the midday rain. The cats
Ate their turkey dinner. She
Screened phone call after
Phone call. A wild loneliness
Descended like a flock of
Robins drained of their red.
Nothing seemed to matter
Anymore, not the past with

Its ax of granite nor the future
With its watery punctuation,
But the moment, yes the moment,
She was forced into it like
So much dough between
The fingers. "God bless us all,"
She said aloud to everyone and no one.
There is no other life.

GNOMON

A mirthy owl stands past breathing.
It is a plate-glass rescue
Of the ten thousand things.
Martha knew it once, came
To her own conclusions.
Then her spirit cried for respite
And release. There was no
Other season for the blatant cross-
Road of the yellow trees.
There was no other, Martha
Knew as she flew to the giant
Warmth in the desert of the real.

PANDORA

Her life seemed a terrible
Nightmare, from which
She was only now waking
Up. She wasn't afraid
Of anything anymore, not
Dependent on any certain
Outcome. She was dangerous,
And when she looked in
The mirror, her eyes sparked
With I'll kill you. Yet she
Had a soft heart, still,
And this was only because
People along the way loved
Her. She was dangerous
Though, would not be controlled
By anyone or anything.

When she lifted the lid on her
Box, it took many years
For the ugly spirits to fly out.
But she found love at the bottom
In the faces of her truest friends.
She hesitated, but only for a second,
Which seemed like an eternity,
And joined her light with theirs.

NO ONE WOULD
BE HOME

Ann finally let go of her
Dead husband. She wrote him
A letter, burned his name in
A candle on her stove,
She took his aftershave
And razor that were sitting
On her dresser and threw
Them away. She then took
His pictures that lined her
Computer desk and put them
All on the dresser. She felt
The need to tell the world,
But now, the world looked
So big, and Ann was small,

Like her name. Would she ever
Find someone new? What
God wills. She wasn't at all
Concerned, but needed to be
Ready to obey. She took
The garbage out and had
Some iced tea. She called
Her best friend and left a short
Message. Dinner was imminent,
And tonight it would not be alone.
She quieted herself, she
Quieted herself, and realized that
When she left, no one would be home.

PERSEPOLIS

Janice rose up like a ruined city.
She defied her limbic system's
Wanton tricks, put something
In her belly and then waited.
Nothing rhymed with ego-death.
The ground was a smoking crater,
And names rose from the ashes
One by one. Janice found her
Own name floating toward her
And she blinked. The smoking
Crater symbolized something,
What she didn't know. It couldn't
Be her heart—that would be too
Simple. Her soul body-slammed
Another soul, as if to say,
I am alive, I've missed myself sincerely.

PHARAOH

"In the spirit and the loudness,
I wipe summer's guilt from
My brow," said Duke.
He cocked the symphony and
Gave it a new wrinkle. What
Once became him started furies,
Then peace beyond peace beyond
Peace. "I am cooking up a stew
So vast and inimitable that
The enemy's hand can't touch it."
Duke had always been given
The brighter side of everything.
Pharaoh, too, made his choices.

FOURTH OF JULY

The sleeper canned his own beans.
"You've made some kind of mistake,"
Ritchie said to him. "You are
A go-getter of roughage, freed
From the demon of grief."
The sleeper's violent angry soul
Was deeply wounded. His big
Brown eyes flickered in the noon-
Day heat. "Whatever floats
Your umbrage, Ritchie," said
The sleeper. "We're drifting,
Endlessly drifting, treading
Water on the sacred ground."
There was a shrinking downpour,
And the sleeper's beans rusted
In the heat. Then, in a mercurial

Instant, there were unimaginable
Sounds, and bright pinwheels lit up
The Fourth of July sky better
Than fireworks. "What do you
Say we get some hot dogs to go
With them beans?" Ritchie asked
The sleeper. "The river, the sun,
And the night will take us
Where we want to go," he replied.
"Hot dogs are for sissies." Then,
Like tired sages, they dropped
Off to sleep and each had the same dream,
That they picked up a tiny blue
Moose and it was smiling.

WELCOME MAT

The whole world clanked like
An iron shovel. "For all my
Talk about complete takeover,
I'm pretty humble," thought
George. A white pigeon flew
Off somewhere. "We didn't
Stand the test of even a little
Time," Mary wrote on a note
To George, pinned it to his pillow.
The note was signed "Mary."
George decided to put an
Umlaut over her name, not
Just one letter, but her whole
Name, one giant umlaut.
George experienced the world
In large strokes from a painter's

Palette, a painter with three ears.
"Even the ice-cream man
Has a plan," sneered George.
Ice cream sounded particularly
Good as a matter of fact, and
George decided to get some.
On his way downstairs, he
Slipped on a banana peel.
His coccyx hurt, but otherwise
He was okay. "If I had anything
At all, I'd give it to Mary,"
George rued. When he saw
The ice-cream man, he busted
His megaphone. "Take that!"
George bellowed. The ice-cream
Man hauled his broken song
Away, leaving a stream of tears.
The sun sidled into Leo.
All was right with the world.

ON BECOMING
A PERSON

Bruno fell in love with his ill-
Begotten self. "Self, I proclaim
You shiny leather, and I love
The way you fit my migration.
Go to it!" His self had other plans,
Unbeknownst to Bruno. When
Bruno found this out, he started to
Cry, and didn't stop for many
Days. The music that came in
Through the window had a great
Beat, and Bruno soon forgot
About his self, and lit a cigarette.
"Self, I banish you from my mental
Kingdom. You brush yourself off

Like a soldier. Your shoes are spit-
Shined and ready, now go and rest."
His self suddenly became angry
And staged a rebellion with bows
And arrows. But then the stars,
The sunsets, made the self wonder
What it was missing. It screamed,
"I should be ashamed, ashamed
Of my attitude!" It was penitent,
But Bruno decided that he could live
Without his self, and so they parted.
When they did, Bruno saw his
Self off in a taxi without headlights.
His self wobbled like a rocking horse
In the cab. Bruno felt an indescribable
Happiness, and went on to save
The world from its self, happy to be
Of service, sad for the miles he had
To go before he slept and slept again.

ERA

The book was a venal stream.
Cassie's hands lay flat upon
Its pages, soaking in the river
From its source. Thunder
Was the order of the day,
And try as she might, Cassie
Couldn't even cower. Her
Face was like the face
Of a clock with its dance
Of Roman numerals. She tried
To wake herself, she tried to
Wake herself, she didn't stir.
The saucepan leaked out some
Milk. She gave it to the cat.
Nothing was wrong anymore

That she could see, and yet,
Her mind raced past itself.
So hard to keep up with the
Synaesthetic air, so hard to keep
Up with the last of last bewares.

RED-EYE

"I'm honored to hold the
High watch for you," Molly
Told Stu. She caught the red-
Eye to meet him. He was
Feeling frail like a tree
That bends in the wind but
Doesn't break. Molly thought
That Stu's life was gray and
Valueless, but still, the nicest
Person you would ever want
To know. But, you have to
Crawl before you can walk,
Thought Molly, and so she
Was showing up for him.
Stu's concerns were ordinary:
How to pay the rent, what to

Have for dinner, love and work.
When they met, Stu kissed
Molly on the lips, and it shocked
Her. But she ignored it, although
He was handsome. "Well,
Stu, I'm afraid we've got nothing
Much to say to each other,
But what are all these toys scattered
Across your lawn?" Stu
Smiled. "Molly, I was looking
For my childhood, and this is
What happened." They kicked a
Red ball back and forth for hours
Until Molly was exhausted.
And so she went back home,
A song lingering, an agony
Played backwards, superimposed
Upon her, and she looked in
The mirror for signs of anguish,
And, not finding any, she slept.

FAVORS FROM
THE DEAD

The dead did Tristan many
Favors. Everything he asked
For, he got. When his talking
Phone was hit by lightning,
He asked his departed uncle Buster
To fix it, and the phone was
Talking again within minutes.
When he asked his great-great-
Great-grandmother to send him
A care package, a fruit basket
Dropped on his head. These
Were only two of the many things
He asked for. When his partner
Died, Tristan found himself being

The lone survivor of an alien race
Of two. His partner had left him
A note, "I leave you my space-
Suit. I will see you again." Tristan
Didn't really know what to make
Of the note, but he started to build
A shuttle in his house. At every
Turn, Tristan asked his partner
For help with the building, and
He got it. When it was complete,
Tristan was excited, and proceeded
To try and launch. But launch, he
Couldn't, and so he asked his partner
For more help. But this time, his partner
Said no. Frustrated, Tristan stamped
His feet and pleaded, but the answer
Was still no. Exhausted from his
Antics, Tristan went into his bedroom
And locked himself in. He crawled
Into his closet as if he were crawling
Into a womb. He noticed something
Shiny in the back of the closet,

And realized it was his partner's
Spacesuit—he really did have one
After all. So Tristan put it on
And fell asleep. He dreamed of
A frozen field of souls, and then
He was one of them. When he tried
To wake up, he couldn't. Tristan
Was ready to acknowledge the magic's
Presence, and so he wandered off
Into the cosmos, searching for
His partner, searching for the light
That he had read about in books,
Which now collected dust on his shelves.

UNANSWERED
QUESTION

"I'm standing on so much wreckage
I think my legs will break," thought
Mary. Mary didn't want anyone
To know she was sad, so she acted
Pleasantly all the time. She had
The thousand-yard stare of a crack
Addict. People thought mean things
About her, like when she was a child
That she'd be barefoot and pregnant by
The age of thirteen, but Mary was
Not discouraged. Mary's whole
World was a giant string of déjà vu.
When she met Roy Willbathe, Mary
Was as happy as a slice of snowy

Cheese. Roy looked like a vulnerable
Sheepdog in drag. Roy told her
Everything she wanted to hear, like,
"I eat my dirty business whole,"
And, "I will bathe . . . eventually."
Roy wouldn't marry Mary because
He said she was too loose. "But
I'm not loose at all, in fact I'm the
Opposite of loose." Roy smiled,
"See ya, kid." And Mary went back
To groping fruit in the market,
Pretending it was the body of a lover,
And eating disgusting things out
Of cans, while the birds chirped quietly
In the dawn outside her kitchen window
After she'd rubbed her wrists with
Scissors oh-so-quietly in the dark.

HOMAGE

She watched him for signs
On how to be. She never
Wavered. She wanted not
To burden him, but burdened
Him anyway. She saw in
Him the will to truth. He
Was like an older brother
To her by his words. She
Considered herself lucky
And wanted to give back,
But how? Twilight fell
Across the ages. A refrigerator
Hummed. There was nothing
Left for her to say or do,
But to become quiet, still
Like wheat in an Ohio summer
Where she had once lived,
Brotherless, dying.

BALLAD

"I never comforted my mother
On her deathbed," he said.
"Of course, she hasn't had
A deathbed yet." And in that
Way it was totally excusable,
And proper and good. No one
Ever told him to change. No
One ever told him he couldn't
Fly. No one ever . . . but it's
All a farce, and it's all bad
Medicine. The trees halted.
One after another, they bent.
Two by two, they caught fire.
They reached this place of safety
And needed to be held like people
Do when they never reach

This place of safety. The
Trees, the winter trees without
Their shawls of dark November.
He sighed. There was no one
Else around to do that, so he did.

RAINBOW LANES

Saskia took a turn for the better.
"I've turned my life into an
Artists' colony, cats run around,
I feel like I'm in a cozy hotel
Somewhere downtown." Saskia
Decided to go bowling, as she
Was drowning in a miasma
Of malaise. She sat down on
A patch of grass outside the
Rainbow Lanes. "Let's see,
There are two farmers for every
One farmer, two cows for every
One cow, but in my infinite
Turpitude I am no longer able
To count how many cows or
Farmers there might be." She

Put on her bowling shoes, which
Were green and red and pink.
She saw a guy she had a crush on,
And he glanced in her direction.
She bowled a perfect split.
She got a glass of beer
From the concession stand,
And decided on her next painting.
The remedial darkness fell.
Saskia was afraid to look outside.
So instead she looked into the void,
And there were rose petals.

A SUBURBAN TALE

The plant was old, sick and frail.
No one came to see it anymore,
And its keeper frequently forgot
To water it. "I think
You murdered it," the keeper's
Wife said one day, jagged
Interloper that she was.
The cat blushed something fierce,
As it had wished the plant dead
Many times, but it had once been
A sturdy plant, so it wouldn't
Be killed by a mere cat.
The plant's keeper left the room
And wept furiously, as he knew
The plant's decline was his fault,

And only his. He decided
To buy a new plant, a prettier
Plant, a girl plant, and he did.
His wife soon noticed his attention
To the new addition to the family
And became jealous. When the keeper
Was sleeping, she cut the plant
Into pieces, and each one crawled
Off in a different direction from
The others, gasping for breath.
When the keeper found out what
Had happened, he had his wife
Beheaded, and he put her head
In a flowerpot and watered it
Every day, combing her wet hair
Out of her eyes. He sang her
Limpid songs, and called her
By her new plant name, Gloria.
"Gloria, I am yours forever,"
He would chant. And it was true.
And they lived happily ever after,

In the shadow of murder, flowering
On its savage, hairy stem,
While the cat grew old and skeletal,
And howled loudly at this laughable
Memento of its nemesis, the plant.

THE LOVE THAT LASTS AFTER DEATH

Many said that Rita was a saint.
She cooked for the poor, talked
To the old, gave her seat on the
Bus up to just about anyone. But
Burt knew Rita was no saint,
As she wrote him every night
With such mercurial self-
Absorption it was hard to fathom.
One day she was happy, the next
Day she was sad. The next day
She was in a rage. Rita wanted
To keep it all contained, so that
None of her ontological horror
Spilled out, poisoning the world.

The days of letters turned to weeks,
The weeks turned to years. Rita
Was too traumatized to stop, and
Always had to keep one step ahead
Of death. Rita imagined death
To be her friend, although she
Really didn't know. One day
Rita decided to wake from her dream
Life and tell everyone how she
Felt, out loud. "I am a satellite
Of blackness, a ship with no sailors.
I don't care if I ever live to see
My children grow up, or whether
I eat pumpkin pie again. I want to
Be dust on the pages of the Book
Of Life." And so she did tell every-
One, but no one understood, as this
Was such a radical departure from
How they saw her, and also they
Were busy, and didn't have time
To grasp the reasons behind
Her confession. The next morning,
Rita sprouted wings like a seagull,

And flew off to meet her long-lost
Love, Emil. Emil had died in a wreck
Years before, but a seagull would
Know where to find him. Emil
Welcomed Rita, told her she never
Had to be human again, that she
Could stay with him forever. It
Was tempting for Rita, but she
Decided to go back into the world
Until it was her time. Burt in his
Infinite patience had always told
Her she would help a lot of people,
And she wanted to try, not in an ersatz,
Distant way, but from the depths
Of her very soul. So Rita tried,
And helped she did. She helped so
Much that she soon forgot about her
Unhappiness and self-absorption,
Although she remained very sad.
Rita finally died an old woman,
Warm in her bed, the moment of
Her death couched in feathers
And Emil's wispy radiance.

DANIEL

He loved the way her hair
Curled in the rain. He
Loved her attachment to
Syzygies. He loved the way
It was always a fat man
Who had keys jangling around
His waist. He loved the sun,
The way a cat loves the sun.
He loved the ruins of old
People ambling down the street.
He loved. And lost. And
Loved again. Numb from
The waist down, there was
Nothing that he didn't love,
Practically speaking. He
Found the sex instinct was

For art and art alone. And
So he made art, and in his
Spare time, he wept. He
Kept away from edges,
Soothed himself to sleep.
He loved the fall, loved to
Rake leaves in the fall.

THE CETACEAN
SOCIETY

The cetacean society was lucky
To have Michael. He came back
From his proton test, and swaggered
In like a giant in their minds,
"I love whales!" he exclaimed,
"Any type of whale! Love 'em."
He hated that sonar stuff, though,
And vowed a long time ago
To end the whales' discomfort
And destruction. It happened to
Be whale mating season, and
This was the society's biggest
Time of year. He could never
Understand exactly how the whales

Did the deed, though, and he was
Too ashamed to ask. He didn't know
Where human babies came from
Either, but he had a vague idea.
He forgot about the existence
Of liverwurst, too, which he enjoyed
With a vengeance, and would
Sometimes feed to the whales.
He imagined the whales sang
To him, and he desired nothing
But to rescue them, from what
He wasn't sure, although at the cetacean
Society, they really thought he knew.

THE IRS

Stanley cheated on his 2001
Tax return, and his 2002,
And his 2003, 2004, and 2005.
He cheated because he felt
Sorry for the government,
And he thought he could give
Them money that way, so that
They could start more wars.
Stanley loved wars, not just
War games, but actual wars
Where men, women and children
Got blown to smithereens.
He didn't know why he loved
Wars so much—he had had
A stable childhood and all,
But wars excited him. One

Day Stanley decided to travel
To a distant shore to start
A war among the natives.
"He called you fat!" and "She
Said you had premature
Ejaculations!" The natives
Were puzzled, as they spoke
No English. Stanley was
Dismayed. Since he couldn't
Manage to start any wars,
He decided to open his own
Dentistry practice on the island.
But no one came to see Stanley,
As everyone used the same
Dentist already, a man with
Wings on his face. So Stanley
Put wings on his face, too,
And people flocked to him
In droves. In time, Stanley forgot
About wars, and became kind.
One day, he was eaten by a tiger,
And went to Purgatory, where he

Was met by an IRS auditor.
"Thank you for helping the war
Effort," the agent said to Stanley.
"But I no longer like wars,"
Stanley replied. "I like teeth."
The auditor smiled at Stanley,
And told him to hush, that he
Had done a good job, and that
Purgatory would only last
For as long as it takes to fill
Out a million 1040 forms,
Minus one rotation of a drill.

IN SICKNESS

"I don't care if she is on a respirator,
I want to go dancing with her," Roland
Cried. Jeanine meant the world to him,
And her brain injury only made her
More attractive. After her car accident,
She became very aggressive, "a raving
Bitch," Roland could attest. Roland
Was smart, but he was ordinary, preferring
Steak to sushi, roads to mountains.
But Roland loved Jeanine, and they mixed
Like water and water. Jeanine failed
To shine Roland's boots properly, but
This was fine with Roland, who got used
To wearing dirty boots. Jeanine in her
Summer clothes was an angel, except
The heat made her retain water and she

Looked fat. She ate popsicles by the
Case, and never once failed to suck
Every bit of juice off the wooden stick.
But now, Jeanine was on a respirator,
And Roland wanted to take her dancing.
Roland sighed. He listened to the leaves
Babbling like lunatics waiting for a dry
Tea kettle to boil, and knitted Jeanine
A sweater. A large sweater, and it took
Him a long time, but it was knitted
With comeuppance and also love.
And they did go dancing in the ward,
Jeanine strapped to a gurney, Roland
On top of the ice-machine box where
Jeanine thought he was trapped inside.

TRUE STORY

Ammonia was Millie's favorite scent.
She'd sniff it for hours on end
Until she was so high that
She passed out. When she awoke,
She'd ride her dog, a giant poodle,
Horticulturally shaved, in circles
Around the kitchen. One day,
She looked down at the linoleum
And saw small animals drawn
In the crevices. "That Booty is
Despicable!" she shouted at her
Dog, who gazed off into the distance.
Booty was her ex-husband who
Ran off with a barmaid. Before
He did, he gave Millie a case
Of crabs. Millie was eighty-

One years old. The barmaid was
Eighty-two. After Booty left
The house, he never came back
Even once, certainly not to draw
Animals on the kitchen floor.
Still, Millie was convinced,
And she went to the police and
Tried to have Booty arrested.
When the policemen came to her house,
They choked on the ammonia fumes.
One of them admonished, "Lady,
All of that ammonia has made you
Screwy in the head." Millie
Was astonished and offended.
She saw the policemen to the door,
And went back to sniffing ammonia
And riding her dog, whose name
Was Muffy. "Muffy, it's just
You and me!" She proclaimed.
The twilight hung in the air.
The animals danced around the linoleum,
Gave Muffy the signal, tore her to shreds.

AUNT LEE WATCHES
THE FIRST SNOW

The children run out screaming
To greet it. I don't
Understand it myself. Can't
They see how slippery it is?
When I was young, I stayed
Inside with my legs up
On the big chair. Instead of
Growing, they withered.
Mama had to wash them for me,
I couldn't look. Now I'm old,
"Older than the vaccine,"
I tell them when they ask.
I let them feel my ankles,
Smaller than the twigs

Of their wrists. Last year,
A girl brought me a snow-
Ball, put it in my freezer
For me. It was still there
Last time I checked, stuck
To the shelf on the door,
Burning white like fever.

THE LAST TIME
SHE SAW HIM

They built a wooden airplane
And painted it with orange
Chrysanthemums, her birth flower.
When it fell, it broke into halves,
One side covered with flowers
And the other a mute blank brown.
They were at the house
The courts designated as a neutral
Place where her father could
See her every Sunday. Her father's fall-
Green eyes changed color
With the colors of the paper
They drew on. He drew mostly
Shapes and she drew beautiful

Women she imagined she loved.
That hot day in June
She kept with her like a tooth
Under her pillow. Her father
And her and her airplane,
Talking about how the leaves
Would fall in October, drunk
With xanthophyll, taping tissues
Dotted red to their faces,
Pretending they were measles.
But then the cab came to take him
Home just as her mother was walking
Up the street to take her home
And he pulled her in. The driver
Started pulling away, one of her
Red leotarded legs still dangling
Out the door. She thought,
Now you've done it, and he had.
She knew through the cloud
Of her parents' struggle that she'd
Never see him again. And as they
Both pulled her, one on her left

Side and one on her right, a police
Car's siren stuck in her like stray
Wires from a fence she tried to jump
Over and missed. She was sent back
Into the house quivering and sinking
Into the muddy-colored afternoon.
She wanted to tell him just one
More thing before the police
Took him. It was that she wanted
Something of his for comfort when
She slept, maybe a sweater she could
Wear and unravel ten years later
And tie into a net before he thudded
Onto the gray littered street from a hotel.
Instead she became a mute six-
Year-old stepping from the front porch
Onto midair, not knowing if anyone
Would be there to catch her
If she ever happened to land.

MARIE

She was the one who noticed
The first forsythias bursting
From their sacs outside her house.
Her brown curls are thinner
Than in the pictures
Taken just a few months before
Beside the horses in the shows,
The moss-grown houses
Of her ancestors, the rising
Shoots of their tombstones.
They talked about her chemo,
The nights she spends throwing up
While her husband sleeps
In front of the TV.
She assures Donna he means well
When he gathers pamphlet
Upon pamphlet on the myths

Of nausea that tell how the sickness
From the treatments can be eased.
She shows Donna more photographs,
This time of her youngest son's wedding.
The baby is coming in July.
In the pictures it is a small snowdrift
Under his wife's white dress.
At the end of their talk,
An old deacon comes to the door.
The week before, he gave her
A statue of Saint Patrick. She
Can tell by the chips in the saint's
Green robe that it is a family heirloom.
She wants to give it back.
But no, he won't take it.
He has come to give her Communion,
Which she takes daily now.
So Donna tells her they'll see each other
Again and she smiles.
Fifty years old, kids gone,
Cradling stiff laughter in her arms,
She smiles at her, as if to say,
A mother of death is still a mother.

LOVE STORY

No job was big enough for Carla.
"I sell jewelry on the beach
In the summertime, I catch fish
With a giant net, I laze about
For days and days, and still I have
More to do." Ronnie piled logs
For firewood, and one day, she
Confessed her love for Carla.
"The sun in your golden hair
Makes you look like a sad sunflower,"
She said, "and I am yours."
Carla was pleased, as she had
Spent many nights dreaming of
Ronnie. "It's okay to do some
Mind-numbing dance, Ronnie.
Now all we need is one of them

Blood-pressure machines and we'll
Be set." Ronnie thought, "This chaos
Is original." She said to Carla,
"Let's live in a blue house together,
Have blue house children, and
Live under the fragile still-
Life of the stars." Carla answered,
"In my dream, I am a slim pixie,
And I dance in the bleak corridor
Of a lost haven. But I am becoming
Too arcane, and all I want is you,
Our blue house, our stars."
And so they did that, and Carla
Dried up like a prune. She hardly
Ever looked at Ronnie, but when
Ronnie died of a liver disease,
She missed her genuinely
And reaped her stellar rewards,
And never again sold jewelry on the beach.

KIND REGARDS

Rex loved apples. Apples were
His life, especially poisoned apples.
He'd scour all the supermarkets
Looking for apples that the dissatisfied
Produce workers had poisoned.
There was a secret code in all of this,
And Rex knew it well. One day
On his way to a supermarket across
The country, he heard a light, buzzing
Sound. A honeybee sidled up to him,
And let out the most earsplitting noise,
A sound much like a buzz saw or
A drill. Rex didn't like being harassed
By a honeybee, so he crushed it
And rolled it around in his hand
Until it was nothing but a fine paste.

He touched a little of it with his tongue,
And discovered that it had the exact
Same aftertaste as a poisoned apple.
Rex was quite pleased with himself,
And turned his car back toward home.
"What do you know about that?"
He thought. He was soon home,
And he turned on the television.
The mayor licked his balls like a dog.
Rex had plans. He dropped off to sleep,
Dreaming of buzzing things, dreaming
Of poison, and making plans that no
One in his right mind would ever understand.

SANDY'S HEROIN

"People were like batteries
To me, then it was all ripped
Away." The sky tore in two,
And tiny people rained down
On her. Their names were
Arbitrary, and she could not
Cop to feeling sad. There
Was nothing stopping their
Virginal hands from feeling
Her empty belly. A thousand
Leaves stuck to an iron tree.
Mistakes were fluent, and knew
No bounds. She found that
Trust is earned, so she went
And earned it, and was clean.

CIRCLE OF LIFE

Nobody loved Jim, but that
Was okay because Jim didn't
Love anybody, either. Jim
Was in a tricycle accident
When he was three. The
Tricycle flipped over again
And again, until its wheels
Melted in the July heat.
Luckily, Jim wasn't on
The tricycle at the time, but
Still, he was traumatized
To see his tiny vehicle go.
Jim's mother was a hag
Who called him names.
She called him names like,
"Sweetie-cakes" and "honey-

Bear." From early on, Jim
Couldn't believe her audacity
And vowed to move away.
And move away he did, far
Far away, so far away that
The sun never shined where
He went. When he was forty,
He came upon a species
Of rare insect, one that crawled
Toward him when he stood
Still. He was fascinated,
And played with the insect
Night and day until it
Withered away and died.
He missed the insect, and
It was then that he decided
To return to civilization.
But civilization would not
Have Jim. Still, he ran for
Office, wrote his own name
On the ballots. One feeble-
Minded person voted for him,

Besides Jim himself. So
He left again in search of
An even better insect, but
Never found one. When
He died, he went to the land
Of butterflies, ate leaves
And flew around. He met
A lady butterfly, and made
Wild, passionate, butterfly
Love to her, and they had
A family. When his daughter
Turned three, Jim got her
A tricycle, and she rode away
Unfettered into the summer night.

ACKNOWLEDGMENTS

Grateful acknowledgment is made to the publications in which these poems appeared: *The Agriculture Reader*: "The West Village," "Protecting the Innocent," "Visiting Hours"; *Bat City*: "Love Story," "On Becoming a Person"; *Conduit*: "These Four Walls," "Noneness," "The Cetacean Society"; *Court Green*: "It Was Freedom"; *Lit*: "Pharaoh," "Persepolis."

I acknowledge and dedicate this book to the following people: Charlie and Barb Wright, Joshua Beckman, Matthew Zapruder, Matt Rohrer, Anthony McCann, Mary Ruefle, Heidi Broadhead, Brandon Shimoda, and the rest of the Wave Books crew.

I also acknowledge and dedicate this book to my parents, Jo-Ann and Jack Sleight,

and Lizzette Potthoff, Soren Potthoff, Hannah Potthoff, Curtis McCartney, Paul Vlachos, Monica Antolik (my sister), Daniel Kramoris, Leah Iannone, Amber Tamblyn, Gordon Ramsey, Walter P. Knake Jr., Liz Whiteside, and Adam Skalman, who especially helped me with creating these poems in so many different ways, it is hard to write about them all.

And Euclid, Timmy, Obi, Marlon, Elko, Topaz,
Minnie, Pearl, SpooDoo, Itchy, and Boots,

and Damon Tomblin—every good and pure
thing I do is a monument to his memory,

and the Creator, who has given me beauty for ashes.